Scottish Pipers

Colin Baxter Photography, Grantown-on-Spey, Scotland

D1379630

Scottish Pipers

Few sights are more stirring – and more instantly recognisable – than that of the kilted Highland piper in full stride. Scotland's piping tradition stretches back over four centuries, and pipes have been used in peacetime, and in warfare. This is music for dancing, and for stirring the soul; for playing on solemn occasions, and for the heat of the ceilidh.

In clan society each chief had a piper attached to his household. Such posts were often hereditary, passing down through generations of families such as the MacCrimmons and MacArthurs in Skye, and the Cummings and MacGregors in the Central Highlands. The piper was expected to lead the clan in battle, and to compose tunes in praise of his chief and other clan dignitaries – the Salutes, Laments, Gathering tunes and clan 'marches' which flourished so brilliantly in the 17th and 18th centuries.

This repertoire of highly stylised tunes, generally played at a moderate tempo, with variations built on a basic theme or ground (in Gaelic ùrlar), became known as ceòl mòr (literally 'big music'). The piper's repertoire also featured dance tunes – jigs, strathspeys and reels – and music which developed hand-in-hand with military use.

Pipes were being played in the kilted Highland regiments by the time of the Seven Years War in the 1750s, but it was from the 1820s, with the introduction of paved roads and the ability to move troops rapidly on the march, that the instrument really came into its own. Tunes known as 'quicksteps' were composed which were designed to put a spring in the step, and enliven the drudgery of the route march. Pipers also served in the front line, and to this day, each Scottish regiment has a pipe band.

The uniforms and parade-ground etiquette of the military pipers passed into civilian use, and, particularly after the end of the First World War, there was a rapid growth in the civilian pipe band movement. Initially such bands were concentrated in the cities and in the mining communities of the Central Belt of Scotland. Many of our most famous bands – such as Shotts and Dykehead – started life in the colliery towns, with the miners putting a penny per week towards their upkeep.

Nowadays the pipe band movement has become truly international, and attracts substantial sponsorship. The World Pipe Band Championship, held each year in August, attracts over 230 bands from a worldwide network of 19 interlinked associations. Recent world champions have come from Canada and Australia, as well as from Northern Ireland and Scotland.

Alongside pipe band competitions there also exists a solo piping circuit associated with local Highland Games. Pipers compete in both pìobaireachd (or pibroch) and march, strathspey and reel events, tapping into a specialist repertoire which evolved during the Victorian period, and which has changed little since. The top solo pipers are the true thoroughbreds of the piping world, often with vast repertoires (all memorised), and impeccable tone and technique.

Another small, but flourishing, aspect of piping culture in Scotland involves the use of bellows-blown instruments which are sometimes known as Lowland or 'cauld wind' pipes. These instruments are much quieter than their larger cousins the Great Highland Bagpipe, and are manufactured in a variety of keys which makes them better-suited to playing with other instruments. Pipes of this type were mainly associated with the town and burgh pipers of the Scottish borders – municipal employees who (in the days before clocks) were expected to play through the town at dawn and dusk, and to perform at feasts and fairs, and events such as the 'riding of the marches'.

The Lowland tradition declined in the 19th century, and much of the music associated with it was lost, but a strong revivalist movement spearheaded by the Lowland and Border Pipers' Society has ensured renewed interest in the instrument since the 1980s. As with Highland piping, the Lowland tradition is now in the very best of health.

Pipe band uniforms reflect the military origins of the modern pipe band movement. Eleven Highland regiments were raised between 1777 and 1794, and it was in these that the pipers first came to play a role in parade ground ceremonial. During the Crimean War (1853-56) each Highland regiment was officially allowed a complement of five pipers and a pipe major, and it was at this time that the pipers started playing regularly with the regimental drummers.

The Highland bagpipe is composed of a blowpipe, bag, chanter and drones fitted with reeds. The pipe chanter has a nine note scale, and the drones provide a fixed accompaniment.

Historically the bagpipe made use of cane reeds imported from Northern Spain and tropical hardwoods such as African Blackwood and Cocus Wood imported from Africa and the Caribbean. Bags were made of sheepskin, treated with specially-made bagpipe seasoning to make them perfectly airtight. Many of the old pipers could make their own reeds, and stitch and tie-in their own bags, but these activities have increasingly become the preserve of specialist makers. In the past 20 years man-made materials have been used to great effect, to the extent that carbon fibre reeds and synthetic bags have become the norm.

The World Pipe Band Championship takes place each year in Glasgow, and attracts over 230 bands from around the globe. The top bands compete in two separate disciplines – the traditional format of the 'march, strathspey and reel', and the modern format of the 'medley'.

Bagpipe music ranges from simple dance tunes to the tradition and splendour of the ancient pìobaireachd.

Highland lore is rich in piping stories. In some old tales, the piper often received his powers from
the fairies in the form of a silver chanter or enchanted reed. In Gaelic, this was known as the *buaidh na pìobaireachd* –
the gift of piping. In other more sinister tales, the piper is lured into a cave, where he is confronted by an other-worldly beast.
As long as he continues to play, he can keep the *uile-bhèisd* at bay, but eventually his stamina must fail, and he descends
into the cave with a cry of *dà laimh 's a' phìob 's lamh 's a' chlaidheamh*. (Oh that I had three hands,
two for the pipe, and one for the sword). And is never seen again.

A top pipe band will have up to 20 pipers and a drum corps featuring a further 10 to 15 snare, bass and tenor drummers. Bands practise hard to play with a high degree of precision, the objective being to make the pipe corps sound like a 'single piper' (albeit a very loud one!)

In Gaelic the bagpipe is known as the 'pìob mhòr' – the big pipe.

Highland Games have been a feature of the piping calendar since the 1820s, attracting the top players to a competition circuit which runs throughout the summer months. For the pipers the 'outdoor' season culminates in events such as the Braemar Gathering on Royal Deeside.

Started in 1950, the Edinburgh Military Tattoo runs for three weeks each summer and is watched by a television audience of over 100 million worldwide. The Tattoo makes use of the magnificent backdrop of Edinburgh Castle to produce a stirring display involving up to 300 performers. Over the years, pipe bands from the Scottish regiments have been joined by musicians from over 40 countries, each bringing a flavour of their own traditions, and producing a spectacle of raw passion and pageantry which is hard to beat.

Highland piping is a living tradition with a rich variety of musical styles. Once confined to Gaelic-speaking Scotland, it now attracts a world-wide audience of performers and enthusiasts. From massed pipe bands, to solo Highland pipers, this is a distinctively Scottish legacy.

First published in Great Britain in 2007 by
Colin Baxter Photography Ltd.,
Grantown-on-Spey, Moray PH26 3NA, Scotland

www.colinbaxter.co.uk

Text by Iain MacInnes © Colin Baxter Photography Ltd. 2007
Photographs © 2007 by:
Marius Alexander: pages 16 top right, 18, 23; Jon Arnold Images/Alamy: page 15;
Colin Baxter: pages 1, 2 left, 5, 8, 9, 10 top and bottom right, 14, 21;
britainonview.com: page13; Doug Corrance: page 16 top left; Courtesy of Edinburgh
Military Tattoo: page 22; Chad Ehlers/Alamy: page 24;

Randall Hyman: pages 2 right, 11, 12, 19; Alan Klehr: back cover; Brian Moyes
Photography / photographersdirect.com: page 6; John Paul Photography: page 20;
Robophotography/Alamy: page 7; Eric Schmidt/Masterfile: page 17; Hugh Sitton
Photography/Alamy: page 10 left; Sportsphoto: page 16 bottom right;
stilldigital.co.uk: page 16 bottom left; Visit Scotland/Scottish Viewpoint: front cover.

ISBN 978-1-84107-353-8   Printed in China